Ten Big Dreams
for
Ten Little Toes

WRITTEN BY ELIZABETH BOBÉ
ILLUSTRATED BY TIARA KINNEBREW

This book is dedicated to my cherished twins, one in Heaven and one here on earth, who have guided me to dream bigger and bolder, beyond what I could ever simply see with only my eyes.

Nicholas,

Although you only rested in my arms briefly, you burst open my heart with an everlasting love. I miss you so much but rest in knowing that I will embrace you again, one day in Heaven.

Sophia,

You are so incredible. Words cannot begin to express how you fill every moment of our lives with joy and laughter. This journey with you has challenged us to believe bigger and see God for who He truly is. You are fierce and have an incredible calling on your life. I am so humbled to be your mommy and have the honor of a front-row seat to the magnitude of the Kingdom that you are impressing upon others. I love watching your story unfold. Don't EVER settle for normal because you, my love, are extraordinary.

Always believe beyond reason.

Love,

Mommy

Oh, sweet girl,
the dreams
I dream
for you.

An endless list.
Here, I'll share
a few...

How about **TEN**??

TEN DREAMS
for TEN TOES?

A magnificent destiny
that the world
yet knows.

Some might
consider this
quite the simple
task...

Toes pushing the
pedals,
wheels whirling
so fast!

Handlebars gripped in
EXCITEMENT
and GLEE,

hair whipping
in the wind,
waving
WILDLY
and
FREE!

These toes
are dressed
fancy to
celebrate
this day.

The day that JESUS
rose; for us,
HE made a way.

Easter basket
in hand,
the egg hunt
is on!

Our hearts
are so filled
as you run
across the
lawn.

And oh,
what a day
when we'll watch

you
plié.

All eyes on
you
as you take our
breath
away.

Could we have
imagined
you'd dance with
such grace?

Your heart surely
knew
by the
look
on your face.

What are dreams
without sand covered
toes, a day full
of waves,

and a sweet
sun-kissed nose?

The sunset and
rising tide
will send us
home soon.

Leaving,
we admire your
footprints
on the sand dune.

The excitement has been
[BUILDING] and BUBBLING
all day.

It's time
to shout,

TRICK-
-OR-
TREAT!!

at every doorway!

These toes are in
costume on
this
whimsical night.

We try to keep up,
yelling,

STAY
IN MY
SIGHT!!

Toes flying
through the air,
higher
and higher.

These swing set
skills weren't
easy to acquire!

But before we
could see your
strength and
your
might,

Your spirit was

fierce,

soaring in flight!

This day, these toes are yet one year older.

Each year as we've watched, you've grown WISER and BOLDER

The cake will be
served with
ice cream in dishes,
but the
SWEETEST treat
today will be
candle-lit

Now these quick toes
are sprinting
in cleats.

We never miss one,
NOT ONE.
of your track
meets.

We'll be in the stands,
holding high
our painted sign.

It curiously reads,

YOU SHOW
THAT
FINISH LINE!

FINISH

These toes will
be dancing
to a

SOFT, SWEET TUNE

How did this
special night
seem to come
so soon?

Prom night, at one time, was only a far-off dream.

Now I kiss your cheek and smooth your sparkly seam.

toes

awaiting to walk
up on stage,

still *em.* NERVOUS

about the speech

jotted down on

your page.

But once you
start addressing
your graduating class,

you remember
these are memories
that will forever last.

These dreams might seem silly, maybe less than grand.

You see, for so many, these dreams are easily planned.

But with our journey,
impossible it may
appear...

but through our journey,
we'll teach the
world
about FAITH,
my dear.

We'll stand strong on these dreams.

Believing, never losing sight.

We will **NOT** be shaken in this <u>MOUNTAIN</u>-<u>MOVING</u> fight.

Not only these
ten,
but more than we could ever
dream;
these toes will do
ALL THINGS,
yes, even the
extreme.

Elizabeth Bobé

Thank you to *God*, first and foremost for putting this story in my heart. All glory be to You! Thank you to my bestie, *Brian Bobé*. You are such an incredible father and husband, and truly support me following my dreams. Thank you to my parents, *Cris Ramirez* and *Elizabeth Robinson*, for always encouraging me to reach for the stars. I think I've caught a really bright one. ☺ Thank you to *Erin Mills* for encouraging me to "go forward and do big things with this book." Your words are always so uplifting. Thank you to *Monte Robinson* and my sister, *Bianca Arroyo*, for helping me express my words just right. A HUGE thank you to the incredibly talented illustrator of this book, *Tiara Kinnebrew*. God truly used you to paint my visions. Lastly, thank you to ALL of those who stand beside us, believing.

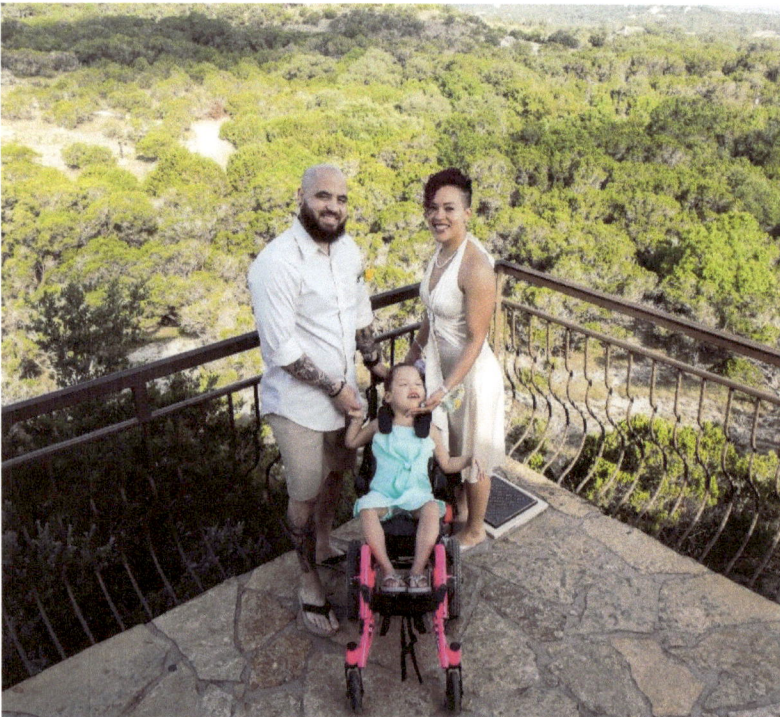

Elizabeth always considered herself a Christian, but not until a turbulent year in her life did she realize she was missing the best part of God's love. Having to forge forward in faith, Elizabeth learned to have, what she terms, "delusional faith," believing when it's beyond reason to believe. She now seeks to spread the hope and faith that she found during that time and every day in each new chapter of her family's journey.

Where to Find Elizabeth (Liza):
Website: www.DelusionalFaith.com
Social Media: * Facebook: @delusionalfaith123
            * Instagram: @delusionalfaith123
            *YouTube channel: Delusional Faith

Tiara Kinnebrew

Thank you to my parents, *Tamiko and Archie Kinnebrew*, for the unconditional love and support through my journey as their daughter and artist; to *Mrs. Bobé* and my *best friends* for the constant encouragement and reassurance; to *myself*, for not giving up on something I fell in love with.

From the age of 5, Tiara has been expressing her ever-growing love for art—music, painting, crafting, and, more notably, drawing. Throughout elementary, middle and high school, she became known for this admiration of hers and somehow developed a reputation for herself as "the Artist." Currently, she is a student at Texas A&M University, pursuing an undergraduate degree in Allied Health. Between her studies and active service with her Xi Delta chapter of Alpha Phi Omega, she spends her time fulfilling commissions and discovering new art styles to use in varying pieces. She feels her absolute love for her craft has been more than rewarding and fulfilling, especially when she's able to lift the hopes, spirits, and joy of its onlookers!

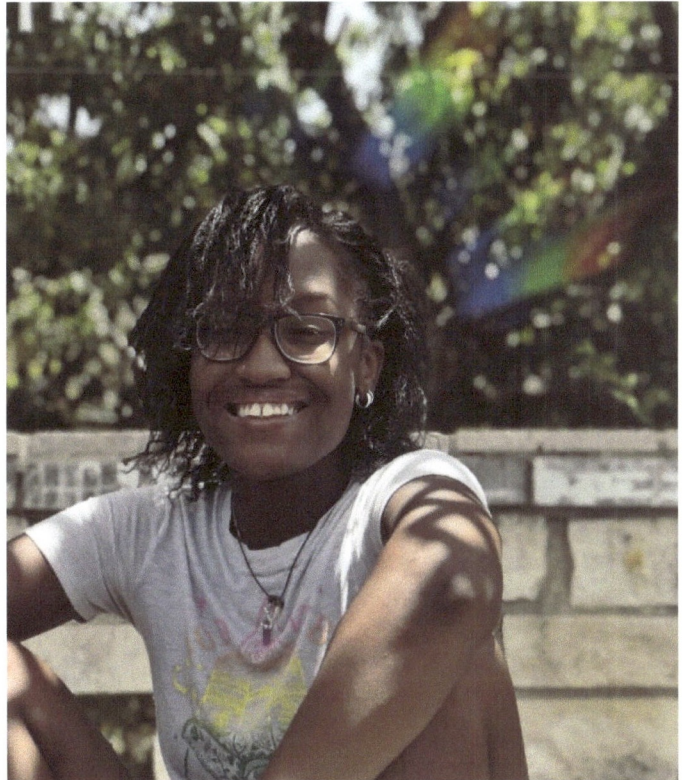

Where to Find Tiara:
Social Media: * Instagram: @kinnewhat
　　　　　　　 * Twitter: @kinnewhat
　　　　　　　 * Periscope: @kinnewhat

Shop for Prints, Decor and Apparel:
　　　　　　　 * RedBubble: kinnewhat